Silk 'Paper' Creations
for the Fibre Artist

Silk 'Paper' Creations
for the Fibre Artist

JUDITH PINNELL

SALLYMILNER
PUBLISHING

To Peggy

First published in 2004 by
Sally Milner Publishing Pty Ltd
PO Box 2104
Bowral NSW 2576
AUSTRALIA

© Judith Pinnell 2004
Design: Anna Warren, Warren Ventures
Editing: Anne Savage
Illustrations: Anna Warren, Warren Ventures
Photography: Bewley Shaylor
Styling: Judith Pinnell and Bewley Shaylor
Printed in China

National Library of Australia Cataloguing-in-Publication data:

Pinnell, Judith.
    Silk paper creations for the fibre artist.

    ISBN 1 86351 336 1.

    1. Decoupage. 2. Silk in art. 3. Decorative arts.
    I. Title. (Series : Milner craft series).

745.546

Disclaimer
The information in this instruction book is presented in good faith.
However, no warranty is given, nor results guaranteed, nor is freedom from
any patent to be inferred. Since we have no control over the use of
information contained in this book, the publisher and the author disclaim
liability for untoward results.

Previous page: Scheherazade turban—beads, feathers and free machine stitching.
The attached mask is beaded and embroidered. The lace-like surface of the
feathered cape is enhanced with beading.

Right: Basket made in bombyx silk using lattice method.
22 cm (8½ in) diameter

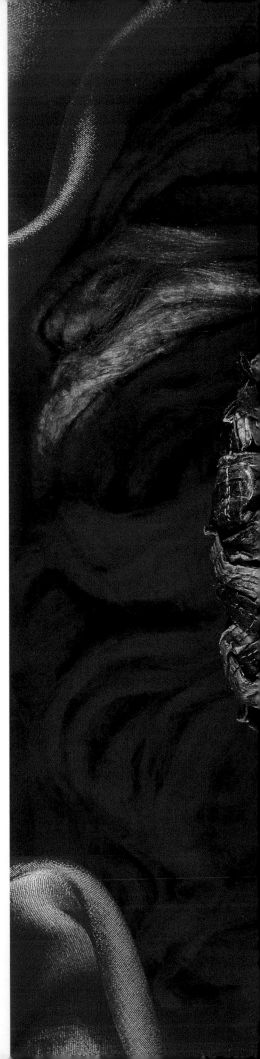

Acknowledgements

- Martin and my family for believing that I could write another book.
- Nancy Ballesteros, for the wonderful silks she dyes that allow me to indulge in my love of colour.
- My friend Jackie Abrams for introducing me to the art of basketry—albeit in a contemporary manner—and inspiring my adventure into weaving the silk 'paper'.
- Contributing artists Sue Seaman, Lois Ives, Nancy Ballesteros and Alvena Hall.
- Peggy Buckingham for her encouragement, and her help with the proofreading.
- Sue Seaman for dyeing the silk chiffon used in the chiffon wrap.
- Lucy for her patience when modelling the garments and millinery.
- To Bewley Shaylor for his wonderful visuals that make the book so colourful.

About the author

Judith Pinnell is a contemporary fibre artist with a passion for colour and texture. Born and educated in Australia, she lived in the United Kingdom for 29 years, where as a mature student she obtained a City and Guilds Diploma in Design and Embroidery. Returning with her family to live in Perth, Western Australia, she began teaching machine embroidery in Perth and country Western Australia.

In the early 1990s Judith 'graduated' to silk 'paper' and found it an exciting medium with which to extend her love of richly coloured textiles. Judith's teaching commitments to silk 'paper' now extend within Western Australia, interstate and New Zealand.

Much of her inspiration comes from the colourful textiles found in India. Over the last ten years she has frequently visited India, and her exploration of the markets, bazaars and villages has given her an eclectic collection of visual material to use in her work.

Take Silk: A Guide to Silk 'Paper' for the Creative Fibre Artist, was published in 2001, introducing this exciting new medium to practitioners in Australia, New Zealand, the UK, Canada and the USA.

With work in private collections, two solo exhibitions—-one in New Zealand, one in Perth—-and articles published in magazines and on a UK website, she is delighted to introduce *Silk 'Paper' Creations* to stimulate those already familiar with silk 'paper' and to entice new devotees to this exciting medium.

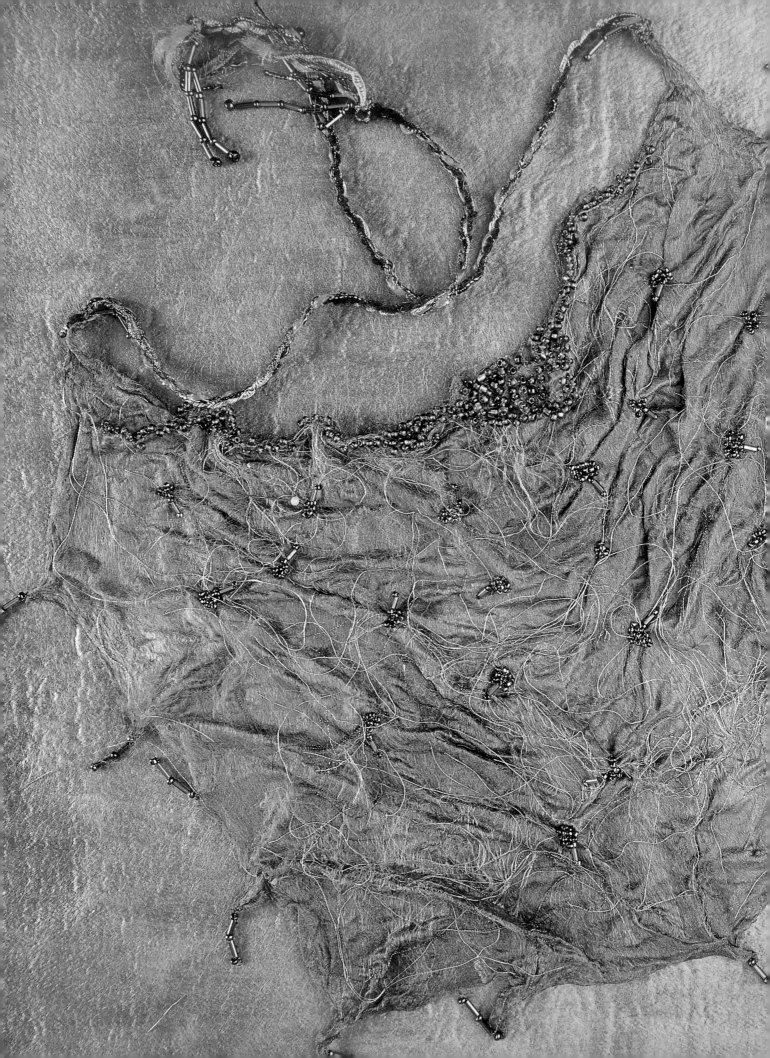

Contents

Collar. The surface of the wet silk was manipulated with fingers to create an interesting texture. Bugle beads were sewn onto the picots formed around the outer edge. Small beads were sewn into the indents when the collar had dried.
23 x 28 cm (9 x 11 in)

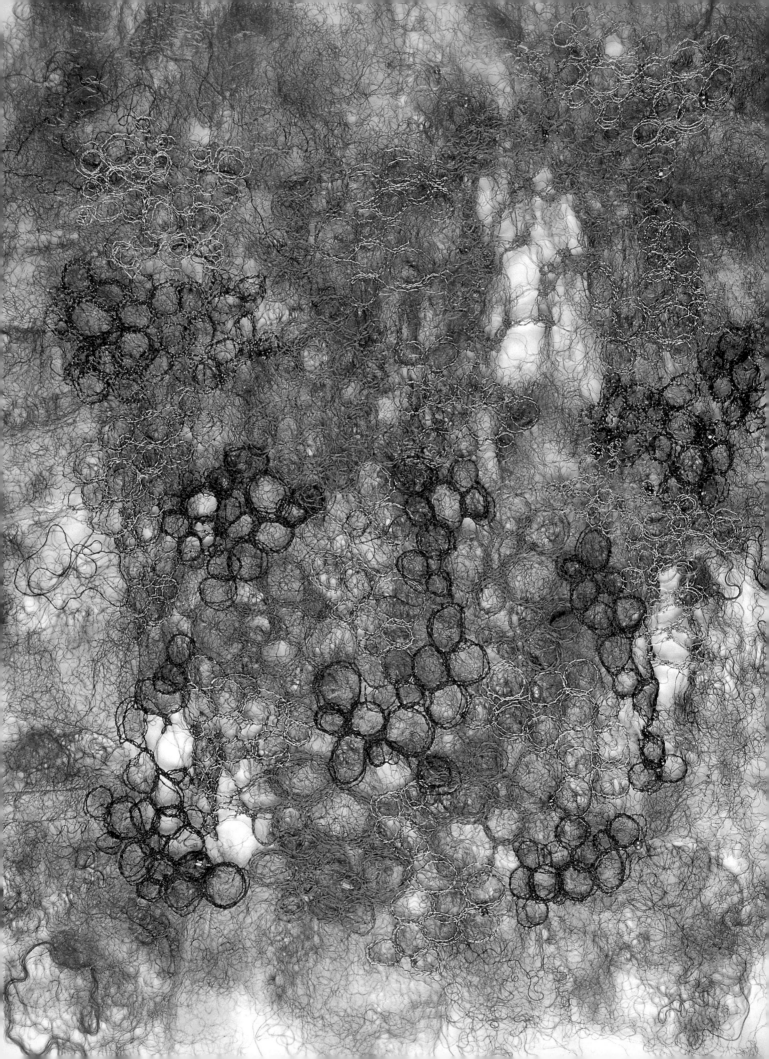

Introduction

In this book we take silk to a completely new dimension, and explore the beauty of silk tops and silk throwster with the various techniques that can be used to manipulate, texture and enhance them.

Silk is lustrous, slightly transparent, and has a beautiful light to it.

Silk is easy to dye, and as a medium for colour there is nothing quite so exciting.

The surface of silk 'paper' is somewhat akin to both felt and paper. The unspun silk fibres make it an extremely strong substrate to work on, using either hand or machine stitching. The finished product is very user friendly and presents a great challenge for the imaginative and creative fibre artist. Unlike wool, however, silk does not felt and thus the most accurate description for the finished product is silk 'paper'.

Silk is a natural fibre and is extremely suitable for dyeing. The rich jewel-like colours, the sensuous feel of the silk, and a desire to create, using rich threads and fabrics as accessories, will present a new challenge for all fibre artists.

Since the publication of *Take Silk* there have been exciting developments in the range of raw silk fibres available. The tussah silk which featured in *Take Silk* has been joined by the very lustrous bombyx silk tops and silk throwster waste—long strands of silk filaments that resemble merino tops and are absolutely fascinating to work and get creative with. These two recent additions are featured in this book, along with innovative new approaches for taking the beautiful silk fibres to exhilarating heights. There will be new enthusiasts to silk 'paper' taking up the challenge to create. Those of you who have already been smitten will find additional avenues to explore and broaden your knowledge for creating with the raw silk.

The range of items that can be produced with the silk 'paper' is extensive: wall hangings, panels, bags and purses, containers and vessels of all sizes and shapes, hats, masks and theatrical accessories, together with wearables and jewellery. Combining the 'paper' with fabrics such as velvet, silk and organza, and embellishments such as beads and feathers, leads to the creation of exciting textured surfaces.

Silk 'paper' is a medium that can be used in almost any aspect of fibre art—whether worked with the sewing machine or by hand, the finished outcomes will delight. Most of my work is done using the sewing machine, but I have found that delicate textures can result by incorporating some of the rich and mouthwatering silk threads that are now available for hand sewing.

By laying down dyed unspun silk tops or silk throwster between two layers of net, wetting down and applying an adhesive/ medium to bind the fibres together, you will have a substrate that will send your creativity soaring to new levels.

If you are searching for rich colours and texture in your work, and would like to experience the excitement of handling pure silk fibres, the techniques included in this book will answer your quest.

About the silks

The silkworm that produces tussah silk, or wild silk, is a native of China and lives on a diet of oak leaves which determines the colour of the silk. Natural tussah is pale cream in colour and a little coarser than bombyx silk, which is produced by the cultivated silkworm. Tussah is easy to pull out when preparing a batt, but because of its cream colouring, the fibres do not dye as vibrantly as those of bombyx. Nevertheless, the finished results are equally stunning.

When wetted down, the surface of a sheet of silk 'paper' made with tussah tops is very pliable and adapts well when used as a single batt to obtain a lace-like surface. Tussah silk can be quilted, manipulated and moulded. The surface of the 'paper' is very receptive to stencilling, using spray paints or textile paints. Appliqué, beading, cut-work and twin needles can also be used to embellish the surface.

Bombyx mori is the domesticated silkworm, which eats mulberry leaves and produces a white cocoon. The silk obtained from the *Bombyx mori* silkworm is white in colour and of superior quality and makes an excellent medium for dyeing. The colours produced are extremely vibrant and rich. The tops of bombyx are finer than those of tussah and require a little more patience when laying down. It is necessary to use a technique called 'snapping' before beginning to work with these tops (see box on page 31).

Opposite: Selection of bombyx silk tops.

Left: Bombyx silk tops.

Throwster waste is formed during knotting and cleaning in the stages of reeling, winding and re-winding bombyx silk. In other words, it is any thread that has to be discarded during the throwing process, and is clean waste. Throwster is different in appearance to both tussah and bombyx and is presented as a ball of long soft fibres rather than a hank—some of the fibres are quite curly, not unlike mohair tops, while others are 'fluffy' in appearance. The fibres are very strong and can be difficult to pull apart when first beginning to work with them. Throwster can best be described as stranded bombyx silk filaments.

Opposite: Selection of Throwster silk.

Left: Some of the vibrant colours available in the Throwster range.

Throwster fibres can be used to achieve an opaque finish or pulled out very thinly to resemble transparent lace. When laying down throwster you do not have to follow the right-angled laying-down technique used for tussah and bombyx. To provide a firm base strong enough to handle and stitch, the fibres need only be presented in a formed network of overlapping fibres.

Tussah, bombyx and throwster are compatible with each other, and can be used together or singly.

What inspires me

The drawings and designs of Erté

The work of this Russian-born Paris-based theatrical designer of the early 1900s has proved an absolute treasure trove of ideas and inspiration—flowing lines that can be used for designing wearable art, garments that seem to have few seams and a proliferation of tassels used in almost everything he made. His designs present the creative fibre artist with a kaleidoscope of choice. Erté's designs feature pockets that are works of art in themselves, motifs that can be interpreted into stylish bags and purses, and elaborate beading to tempt any novice. As a source of design ideas for hats, hems, bags, wraps and exotic costumes, his work exudes inspiration and ingenuity.

The prayer flags of India

These were the inspiration for the hangings right, on opposite page and page 20, constructed from silk tops and throwster. In Sikkim, prayer flags hang majestically from tall poles on the roads that lead to the monasteries. Prayers are printed on the flags, and the Tibetans believe that when the lettering fades away, the wind has carried their prayers to be heard by the gods. There are also small flags in primary colours that are festooned across the streets and doorways on festival occasions. These small ones add so much colour to the houses and streets and are one of my

Above: Orange/yellow hanging. Bombyx and throwster silk manipulated with a satay stick before wetting down. When dry, the silk was beaded. The Textile Medium used to bond the silk fibres was slightly watered down to give a softer feel to the hanging. Inspired by Tibetan prayer flags.
114 x 62 cm (45 x 24½ in)

Opposite: Cerise/pink hanging.
114 x 62 cm (45 x 24½ in)

Above: Cerise/wine hanging. Bombyx and throwster silk manipulated with a satay stick before wetting down. When dry, the silk was beaded. The Textile Medium used to bond the silk fibres was slightly watered down to give a softer feel to the hanging. Inspired by Tibetan prayer flags.
124 x 58 cm (48½ x 23 in)

Right: Green/blue/lime hanging.
114 x 62 cm (45 x 24½ in)

strongest visual memories, inspiring me to use similar bright colours in my work. Their hues of red, green, yellow, blue and white, with imagination, can be used in a variety of ways.

Materials and equipment

To make silk 'paper' you will need:

- Flat working area big enough to accommodate the sheet of plastic used to prepare the batt

- Sink and water close to the working area

- Sheet of strong plastic at least 1 m (1 yd) square; this should be larger than the estimated size of the finished 'paper' (hardware shops are a good source)

- Nylon net, approx. 2 m (2 yd) to begin with, any colour (I prefer black); tulle is not suitable as it tears when it is removed from the dry silk

- Selection of silk tops and throwster

- Adhesive/medium solution

- Rubber gloves and apron (optional)

- Washing-up liquid (see below)

- Two household paintbrushes, 5–8 cm (2–3 in) to apply water and medium

- Sponges or old towels, for mopping up excess water and soap suds

- An iron, ironing cloth, brown paper or transparent baking paper

- Hairdryer, to be used when moulding bowls and three-dimensional items such as masks and containers

- Two or three yoghurt pots or takeaway containers to hold soap/water mixture and adhesive

- Selection of glass or plastic containers of interesting shapes and sizes suitable for moulding the silk (please, not your best acrylic containers, as they can be stained by the medium)

- Drying frame (see below)
- Bucket beside the sink, useful for washing out the net after use

Washing-up liquid/detergent

Unlike wool, silk does not felt and therefore the fibres must be adhered together in some other way to make the silk 'paper'. Wool has minute hooks on the fibres that enable it to felt when wet, but silk fibres are smooth and require the presence of an adhesive to bind them together.

Before painting the surface with the adhesive/medium, it is necessary to apply a solution that contains a gentle chemical detergent, such as that found in washing-up liquid. This penetrates the silk fibres and allows the bonding solution to work between them.

The strength of different brands of detergent varies, so experiment with the one you intend to use to find the quantity required. (*Note*: Some ecologically safe detergents do not open up the fibres sufficiently to allow the bonding solution to penetrate.)

Net

The net allows you to 'paint' the detergent solution and bonding solution onto the dry silk without disturbing the carefully prepared batt.

Opposite: Equipment for making the silk 'paper'—sheet of thick plastic, coarse net, paintbrushes, silk tops and silk throwster, cloths/sponge, two solutions, washing-up liquid, drying frame, containers for medium and washing-up liquid and water.

Adhesives/mediums

You will find that there are many textile adhesives/mediums on the market—in fact the range can be quite bewildering when you begin to look for a suitable one. Each has its own special component that may or may not be suitable for use with the raw unspun silk.

After working for some time with Nancy Ballesteros, who dyes the beautiful silks I use, we established that the two bonding solutions I use give the most lasting results but at the same time do not detract from the beauty of the raw silk.

Jo Sonja's Textile Medium

This medium, made by Chroma Acrylics, will leave the surface with a water-repellent finish. Silk 'paper' made using this medium is suitable for wearable art, bags, purses, book covers and wall hangings, in fact, anything that will be frequently handled. As 'paper' made using Textile Medium is not as stiff as that made using Acrylic Gloss Medium (see below), it is not suitable for making items that you require to be freestanding. It is not necessary to use a machine embroidery frame when working free machine embroidery on 'paper' made with Textile Medium.

Once the silk has dried it is important to iron it beneath a press cloth, brown paper or transparent baking paper, using a medium-to-hot iron to seal the surface, prior to embellishing the 'paper'. Ironing the dry 'paper' leaves the surface water repellent.
The finished 'paper' has a slightly coated feel to it, is flexible, lustrous and resistant to rubbing. Remember, because you are using silk fibres a small amount of rubbing may occur.

Always follow the manufacturer's instructions, but, as with all mediums, you can experiment and dilute it to obtain a softer but not necessarily less stronger 'paper'. Textile Medium is not usually diluted when used for general purposes. Should too little medium be applied, the layers of the finished 'paper' will separate.

If you are making 'paper' using throwster, however, and would like the surface to be delicate and almost transparent, then you can dilute the Textile Medium a little.

It is wise to experiment with the proportions of medium and added water for specific projects. To control the degree of dilution, add water to the Textile Medium using an eye-dropper.

Textile Medium leaves a water-repellent surface so it is not possible to add more solution to the dry 'paper' to correct any fibres that may be 'unglued'. You can often rectify a fuzzy surface by reinforcing the 'paper' with hand or machine stitching over weak areas. Applying more solution when the 'paper' has dried will leave a watermark.

Should 'paper' made with Textile Medium become stained, it can be gently wiped with a damp cloth.

Atelier Acrylic Gloss Medium and Varnish

Also made by Chroma Acrylics, this produces a stiffer 'paper' ideally suited for sculpting articles such as bowls, boxes and masks.

This product is diluted 50/50 with water. As before, however, follow the manufacturer's instructions. As with the Textile Medium, you can experiment with the proportions for specific projects.

Although the finished 'paper' is stiffer than that made with Textile Medium, it is still receptive to stitching, either by hand or machine, and free machine embroidery can be worked without using a frame.

If the dry 'paper' has a fuzzy appearance in places, this means the Acrylic Gloss solution has been unevenly applied. Simply brush on a small quantity of solution and leave to dry. It is not necessary to replace the net. If there are large areas of loose fibres, you will need to brush on a small quantity of water before brushing on more solution. Leave to dry, then press to remove any ripples.

Should you wish to add more dry silk to an existing piece of 'paper' made using Acrylic Gloss, apply a small amount of water to soften the dry surface, add the silk, replace the net and finish with plain water and more solution. Replace the net and leave to dry on the frame.

For a rigid surface, fast-dry the wet silk with a hairdryer set on medium/high. Use this method when shaping over a form or bowl, or when making masks. Dry the work over a thick pad of newspapers placed on the work surface. These will soak up the excess liquid. Any project intended to be freestanding will benefit from drying with applied heat.

Acrylic Gloss and Textile Medium are not compatible and cannot be mixed together.

Tussah, bombyx and throwster silk are all suitable for use with Textile Medium and Acrylic Gloss, although experiments have shown that throwster does not respond to the Acrylic Gloss as well as tussah or bombyx. It is not possible to obtain enough rigidity to enable a receptacle or container to stand independently.

There are other mediums available that can be used to bond the silk fibres but I found the results were not aesthetically pleasing, nor was there the permanency obtained through the use of Textile Medium or Acrylic Gloss. Nevertheless, the bonding medium you use will be a personal choice, so experiment!

Spray starch will also bond the fibres, but gives better results when felting silk together with wool tops.

Bonding powder, a glue that comes in a fine powder form, is a good medium to use when bonding silk 'paper' motifs to a background fabric such as silk, organza or chiffon. You simply arrange the dried motifs made from either of the silk tops in your chosen pattern on the fabric and pin them in position, placing the pins vertically. Lift the first motif and sprinkle a small quantity of bonding powder on the background fabric. With an ironing cloth or clear baking paper to protect the iron plate, carefully press the motif to the fabric with a moderate to hot iron. Repeat the process for each motif, overlapping some of them to add texture to the surface.

Methylcellulose, used by papermakers, will not give a permanent finish to the silk fibres and is really only useful if the work is to be heavily stitched, used in conjunction with wool felting, or mounted under glass. This is primarily a size that comes in powder form and can be thinned or thickened. It leaves a thin film on the surface of the silk 'paper'.

Drying frames

The wet silk should not be left on the plastic to dry. It will accumulate excess solution and leave a shiny surface that will mask the beauty of the silk.

The frame you use to dry the silk should allow the water and solution to drip freely through a mesh-type base.

When you first start to make silk 'paper', a cake cooling rack can be used for small pieces. Once your pieces become larger, you will find a frame similar to a screen-printing frame more useful—-but it is not a good idea to use an actual screen printing frame, as it will become clogged with the adhesive.

A simple homemade frame can be constructed from 40 x 20 mm (1¾ x ¾ in) pine stapled together at the corners. Fine nylon netting is then stretched over the frame and attached with staples. I find a frame measuring 52 x 72 cm (20½ x 28½ in) a handy size for general use.

Should you wish to create wearables or large wall hangings, a larger drying frame will be necessary. For garments and banners I use a frame measuring 2 x 1.5 m (6 x 4½ ft). When I use a frame for large pieces of work, the ends of the frame are supported above the ground by a pair of trestle stands, enabling the wet silk to drip dry.

Making silk 'paper' from tussah and bombyx

If this is your first attempt at making silk 'paper', just follow these simple instructions, which will enable you to make a sheet of beautiful 'paper' on which to create a very individual piece of work. Throwster requires a somewhat different technique, described on page 45.

1   Gather together the silk tops, plastic sheet, net, solution, detergent, paint brushes, containers for solution, and rags/sponges. Access to water is an advantage.

2   Lay the plastic sheet on the work surface, smoothing out any wrinkles.

3   Cut two squares of net. These should be at least 7–10 cm (3–4 in) larger all round than the estimated finished piece of 'paper'. Each piece of silk 'paper' will have a piece of net on the front and back which will be removed when the silk has dried. Place one piece of cut net on the plastic.

4   When laying down the silk, keep the working area completely dry.

Before wetting down the silk fibres ensure any remaining unused silk has been put to one side to prevent it getting wet.

Preparing the silk tops

1   Place one piece of the cut net on to the plastic.

2   It is easier to work with short lengths of silk. A workable size is 26–38 cm (10–15 in) so free this amount from the hank of tussah. Grip the free end in your right hand and the long end in the left hand. With your hands approximately 12–15 cm (5–6 in) apart, gently pull away a length of the silk. Another method of preparing the silk tops for laying down, is to lay one end of the tops on the table and place the right hand firmly over the ends of the silk. With the long length of silk held about 15 cm (6 in) away in the left hand, gently pull away the silk fibres. Reverse the procedure if you are left-handed. If you are working with bombyx, before beginning to pull the fibres apart, use the technique referred to as 'snapping'. See the box below.

Snapping An explanation of the difference between pulling tussah and pulling bombyx.

Tussah is wild silk and coarser than bombyx, therefore the tops are thicker, which is what makes it easier to 'pull out'.

Bombyx is finer and stronger than tussah, which is why it is necessary to gently 'tug' the fibres before laying them down. The tugging or snapping ('snapping' is the correct term) releases the fibres from each other and makes it easier to pull them out.

Using both hands, gently pull the fibres to the left and right at the same time.

3   The silk will pull apart easily and a piece approximately 1–1.5 cm (½ in) wide, and 12–15 cm (5–6 in) long, will be ready to work with. If the silk has been hand dyed, the fibres may require a few gentle pulls to loosen them.

4   Some static electricity may develop during this process; this can be alleviated by lightly spraying the silk with an anti-static spray, the type used on synthetic fabrics to prevent them clinging to the body. The spray can be found in department stores (refer to Anti-static Spray). Wait 6–7 minutes for the silk to dry, then continue preparing the batt.

Laying down the silk tops

If you are preparing 'paper' to make an item that requires a flat, smooth surface, such as a book cover, purse or wall hanging, you will need to lay down the silk in a very controlled, neat manner to ensure that the 'paper' will be strong in all areas.

The nature of the item you are making will determine how many layers are required. For a lace-like surface, one layer is sufficient. To make items that will be handled a lot, the 'paper' will need to be stronger, and two or three layers are recommended. It is not necessary to make the 'paper' any thicker than three layers. It is better to make three thin layers rather than two thick ones.

1   Lay the lengths of silk on to the net, working across in rows
    from left to right (reverse this if you are left-handed), and
    ensuring that each length lies closely butted to the one next
    to it. This will assist in retaining the strength of the 'paper'.
    Second and subsequent rows across will overlap the one
    above by approximately 3–5 cm (1½–2 in).

2   Leave a border of net approximately 5–7 cm (2–2½ in) wide
    all around. If the tips of the silk fibres extend beyond the
    net, the paintbrush tends to catch these wisps, making it
    difficult to keep the silk in place when wetting down.

3   The second layer is placed at right angles to the first one,
    that is, if the fibres in the first layer run vertically, those of
    the second layer will run horizontally.

4   The third layer will lie at right angles to the second layer,
    making a sequence of vertical, horizontal then vertical.
    Laying down the fibres in an orderly manner will result in a
    high lustre. Place the second piece of net over the prepared
    batt.

1. Place the plastic on the work surface.

2. Cut the net to size and place one piece of net on the plastic.

3. Begin preparing the batt by laying the silk in horizontal lines.

4. The first layer is illustrated. This picture also illustrates one of the methods for 'pulling out' the silk.

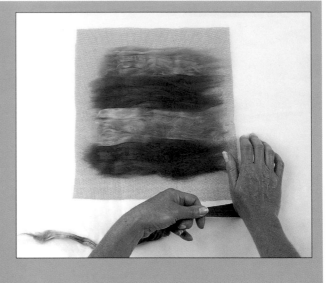

5. When adding a second layer, lay it at right angles to the first layer.

6. If a third layer is required, this will be laid at right angles to the second one. This picture illustrates a second method of 'pulling out' the silk tops.

7. Lay the second piece of net on top of the prepared silk.

8. Using a paintbrush, thoroughly wet both sides of the prepared silk, with the washing-up liquid and water mix, mopping up any excess as you go along.

9. Apply the bonding solution to the wet silk on both sides, and move silk and net to the drying frame.

Wetting the silk

The fibres of the silk must first be separated to enable the medium to penetrate and adhere them. The chemicals in the detergent will allow the medium to be absorbed.

1   Put approximately 1 teaspoonful of detergent into a container, and add 300 ml (10½ fl oz) of water. Adding the detergent first enables you to determine how much is required to make a reasonably soapy mix. Gently agitate the water, using the paintbrush to distribute the detergent evenly.

2   Using the paintbrush, apply the detergent mix through the net onto the silk, using strong strokes. This is an important stage in the formation of the silk 'paper' and the detergent mix needs to be well worked into the silk. Do not be concerned with the amount of lather on the net at this stage, just mop up any excess with a sponge. Neither detergent nor medium will be visible when the silk has dried.

3   Turn the silk and net over and thoroughly wet the second side. Remember, it is very important to wet both sides of the batt. Now wash the brush clean of detergent before applying the medium.

Applying the medium

The adhesive you use will be a personal choice, but I find the best results come from Jo Sonja's Textile Medium and Atelier Acrylic Gloss Medium.

Normally, the Textile Medium is not diluted. If, later on, you plan to experiment by watering it down, a very soft and light piece of silk 'paper' will result. Diluting the Textile Medium hardly detracts from the strength of the finished 'paper', but it will be very delicate and look quite transparent.

The Acrylic Gloss is diluted 50/50 with water for general use, but, as with the Textile Medium—experiment.

Silk 'paper' made using Textile Medium must be ironed prior to being embellished. Pressing the 'paper' using a medium/hot iron seals the surface, rendering it water repellent.

1   Using the medium required for your project, and following the manufacturer's instructions, apply it to both sides of the wet silk and net. Both mediums are white and opaque, which makes it easy to ensure that all the surface has been covered. It is important to apply the medium evenly so that the fibres bond together and the layers of the dry 'paper' will not separate later.

2   When applying medium, the brush will collect excess detergent from the wetted silk, so pour only a small quantity into the container at any one time. This cuts down the

amount of excess detergent being transferred from the brush
to the medium mix.

3   To move the wet silk and net to the drying frame, fold the
plastic sheet towards the centre and carefully lift the
contents. This method ensures that no liquid is spilt.
Carefully lift the wet silk and net from the plastic and lay it
on the frame, then gently smooth out any wrinkles with
your hand. Do not place the frame in direct sunlight, as this
will damage the silk. Do not leave the silk to dry on the
plastic—this leads to a build-up of detergent and medium
that will leave a glossy surface that detracts from the beauty
of the silk 'paper'. Drying times will depend on the climate.
In a warm atmosphere a three-layered sheet of 'paper' will
take about 12 hours, in a cooler climate approximately
18 hours. Thin sheets of 'paper' will dry in about 4–5 hours.

4   Clean down the work surface, brushes and containers. If a
washing line is available, peg the plastic to the line and hose
off the remaining solution.

The final step

The silk must be totally dry before the net is removed. To test if
the 'paper' is completely dry, gently pull away a corner of the net,
peeling it away in the direction the last layer of fibres was laid
down. If the net sticks to the silk, leave to dry a little longer and
test again before removing the net from both sides of the 'paper'.

Wash the net and remove any silk fibres. The net can be used
several times.

Manipulating and texturing the surface

Once you have familiarised yourself with the technique of creating flat sheets of silk 'paper' you will begin to think of ways the silk can be manipulated to transform the surface from a flat one to one with textural qualities.

Again, begin your experiments with bombyx or tussah rather than throwster, which requires a different technique (see page 45).

For initial experiments with manipulation, start by preparing a sheet of 'paper' in the usual way, using Acrylic Gloss, which produces the best results when texturing. Textile Medium can be used but the stiffness that results will not have the body you will get when using Gloss Medium.

I usually make a piece approximately 30 cm (12 in) square when trying out new surfaces, which becomes part of my extensive folio of samples which I find invaluable when developing new surfaces and textures. (Samples larger than this take up too much space.)

Opposite: Pink and green bombyx silk tops thinly laid and bonded using lightly diluted Textile Medium.

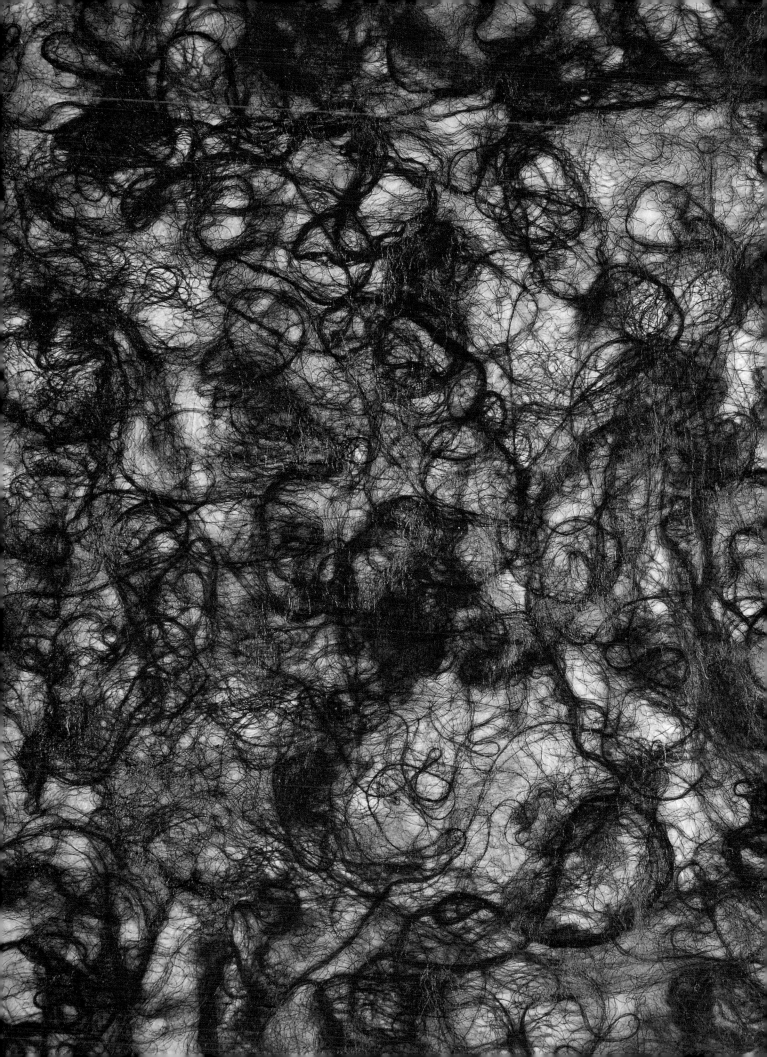

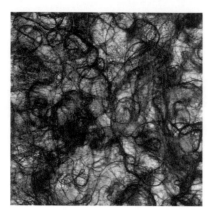

Once the silk fibres have been wetted down they become pliable, strong and manageable, and it is then very easy to texture the surface before drying. The usual procedure when preparing a sheet of 'paper' is to leave the batt between the layers of net to dry, but for a textured surface you need to remove the net from both sides before reshaping the wet, pliable silk fibres with your fingers. You then carefully transfer the silk to the drying frame. You may lose some of the texturing when moving it, but it's easy to restyle. Then leave to dry in the usual way.

The finished result will depend on whether you have made a one-, two- or three-layered piece of 'paper'. A thin single layer of silk will produce a delicate, almost transparent piece which can be embellished with stitching, either by hand or machine. If it is fine and delicate the work will require a little more care and patience when handling, but the end result will be well worth the time spent. Two and three layers of silk have more body and are therefore much easier to work with but will take longer to dry.

Embellishing the surface

If you wish to combine machine or hand embellishment with a manipulated surface, the embellishment must be done first.

Make the 'paper' using Acrylic Gloss as the medium. Dry the silk 'paper' still sandwiched between the net on the drying frame. When completely dry, remove the net from both sides.

Work any decorative stitching required, either by hand or machine. You can also embellish with beads, appliqué or any other chosen method of decoration.

Return the work to the plastic sheet and wet the 'paper' using a small amount of water only, followed by a small amount of Acrylic Gloss medium. The embellishments can also be wetted down without risk of damaging stitching or beading.

Proceed to manipulate and texture the surface to the desired shape and leave on the frame until completely dry. For a more rigid surface, dry completely using a hairdryer set on medium/high. This method can also be applied when making masks.

Working with throwster extends the challenge of texturing 'paper'—see the next section.

Checkerboard bag. One side of the bag is made of silk 'paper', the other of cotton velvet. The strap is velvet. The beads add highlights to the tiny squares of silk 'paper'. These small shapes were adhered to the background of vilene with Vliesofix prior to stitching. A beaded fringe completes the rich appearance of the bag. The lining of silk fabric was hand stitched to the inside of the bag. This is a simple exercise in combining rich velvet with the beauty of silk 'paper'. 24 x 19 cm (9½ x 7½ in) including beaded fringe

Moulding silk 'paper'

The technique of moulding is suitable for tussah and bombyx silk tops, and the 'paper' is made using Acrylic Gloss medium. This is the solution that gives body to three-dimensional projects and makes the silk suitable for moulding. The technique can be used for masks, bowls and other containers.

After the silk has been wetted down with the detergent and solution, remove the net from both sides and prepare for drying in the shape of your choice.

The shape or form that you choose to mould the wet silk on will not necessarily be the finished shape. It is not advisable to use your good plastic containers (they will be discoloured by the solution). Experiment with jars, ice-cream containers (for larger pieces), flower containers, sweet bowls, unusually shaped shells. Seek out chain stores and second-hand shops for unusual shapes. The form acts as a base on which the silk rests while it is being dried with a hairdryer. It can be dried on the inside or the outside of the form; the shape will be bigger if moulded over the outside. It is suggested, however, that you make your first moulded project with the silk on the inside of the form.

Opposite: Simple bowl made in bombyx with an insert of throwster. A wet batt of bombyx was moulded over a simple form and shaped using a hairdryer until it was completely dry. The inner shape of throwster was made by the same method. This is a good starter project for combining bombyx and throwster silk together.

Before beginning to dry the wet silk, lay a thick pad of newspaper on the work table to soak up excess liquid. Stand the form and the wet silk on a jar set on the newspaper pad. This lifts the work above the table surface and makes it easier to dry all of the form. Using a hairdryer set on medium/hot, held about 20 cm (8 in) away from the silk, begin the drying process. If you are using a form with a textured surface to produce a textured surface on the silk, press the silk into the hollows on the form as you go along. The shape can be changed as you work, and you may find that your finished piece is very different to the one you originally envisaged. Remember to turn off the dryer from time to time to prevent it overheating.

Depending on the size, and the thickness of the silk, drying time can be up to 2–3 hours.

Rhapsody in Blue
27 cm square x 14 cm deep (10½ x 5 in)
Bombyx silk, basket technique.

The beauty of this technique is that if you do not like the finished shape, the dry silk can be wetted down with water, then more solution, and totally reshaped. This can only be done when Acrylic Gloss medium has been used.

Examples of this technique include the basket on page 4, the vertical vase on page 69, the simple bowl on page 43, 'Rhapsody in Blue', left, and the tulip bowl on page 100.

Throwster—
the finer points

Working with throwster requires a different approach. 'Paper' made with tussah and bombyx is opaque, but when it comes to using throwster, transparency takes over.

Once you have mastered manipulating the tops, the challenge is to experience the delicacy that throwster presents. This also incorporates the use of colours and how a metamorphosis can eventuate by using fibres so fine that overlaid gossamer sheets of throwster actually take on a myriad different colours. Throwster is very susceptible to static so an anti-static spray will be useful to control the fibres.

Here are some exercises using throwster that show the versatility of this particular fibre.

Using transparent fabrics as a permanent base

With the net as the working base, lay down any one of the following: chiffon or organza, in either silk or rayon, metallic or plain net. There are also organzas with metallic flecks, and fabrics woven from metallic threads.

Sample. Purple throwster on multicoloured metallic net, block printed using metallic textile paints when dry.

Opposite: Sample. Purple throwster on multicoloured metallic net, block printed. The metallic net is visible beneath the throwster fibres.

Below: Sample. Gold/orange throwster on gold metallic net.

Lay down the plastic, then the net, then your chosen background fabric, and proceed to lay down a fine layer of throwster. This can be in the form of motifs or an all-over piece. Gently pull small pieces of throwster from the ball and lay it down randomly in its naturally curly form; it will not form straight lines like bombyx or tussah. Depending on your project, the fibres can be laid sparsely or a little more thickly.

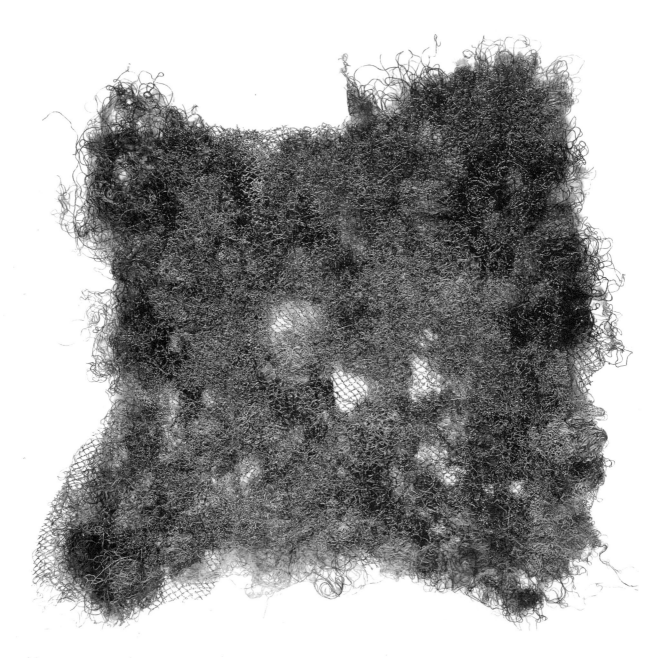

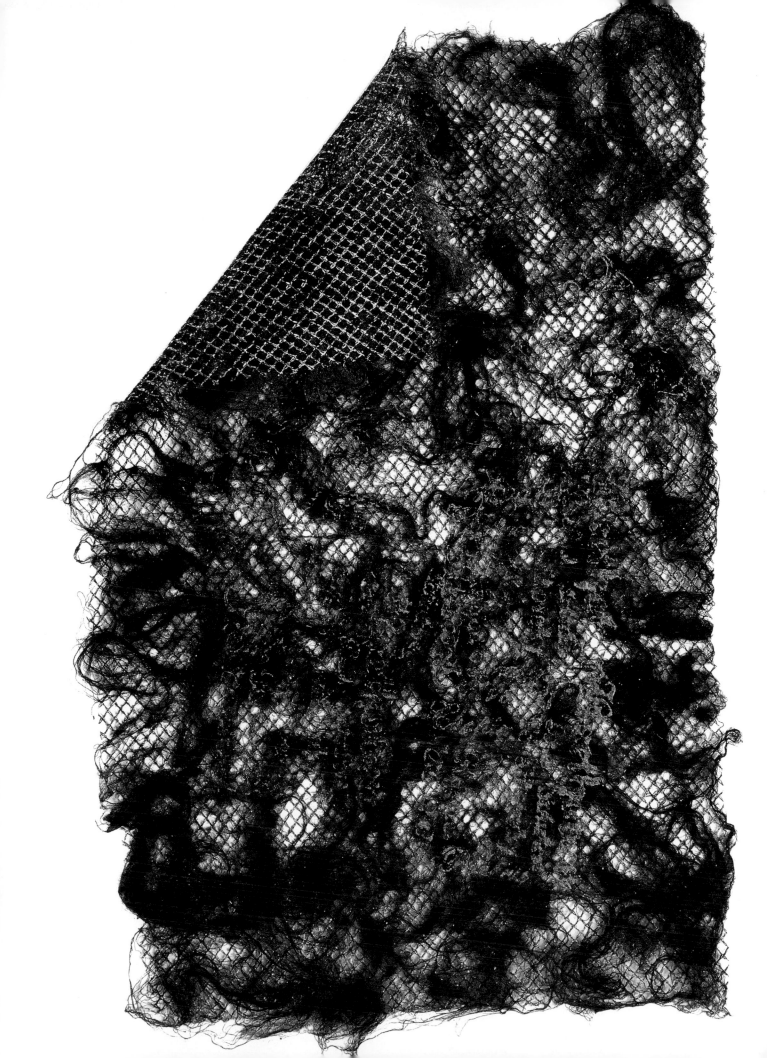

Place a piece of net on top of the fibres when you have a pleasing pattern. Wet down with water and detergent on both sides. Lightly dilute some Textile Medium with water using an eye-dropper and apply with a brush, as for tussah and bombyx, to both sides of the throwster and the chiffon or organza. Leave to dry on a frame. The fibres will dry quickly. When dry, carefully lift the net from both sides. The chiffon or organza remains as a base adhered to the throwster.

Throwster will adhere very well to silk fabrics, but not as securely to rayons and synthetics. This is not a problem—just add some extra free machine stitching to keep the fibres in contact with the background. Add a sprinkling of beads to highlight the work.

Because the fibres of throwster are very fine but strong, using full-strength Textile Medium is not necessary. I have found that only a small quantity of medium is required to form the fibres and enable them to be contained. Refer to samples on pages 45 and 46.

Opposite: Yellow/gold bombyx bonded onto purple silk organza background.

Applying throwster motifs with bonding powder

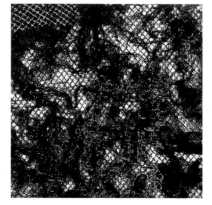

Using throwster, prepare motifs which can be used randomly or as a border. Use a slightly diluted Textile Medium and the method described above.

If your project calls for a border, to avoid having to hem the end of a fabric such as silk organza or chiffon, sprinkle a tiny amount of bonding powder on the placement for the motif, and place the motif on the bonding powder.

With the iron on medium to hot, place a small sheet of transparent baking paper or brown paper between the iron and fabric and motif. Using transparent baking paper will make it much easier to determine the placement of the motif. Carefully press the motif to the fabric. It can be positioned slightly over the end of the fabric or just above the edge. Try overlapping some to add texture and interest.

With machine embroidery thread in the bobbin and on the spool, set the machine for free machine stitching using the darning foot. Stitch freely over the bonded motifs. With care, it is possible to stitch without using a frame. This prevents the organza or chiffon being creased. It is not necessary to cover the motifs with stitching, add just enough to ensure they are secure.

To complete the embellishment, beads, either contrasting or toning, can be added. Once the decorative finish is complete, carefully cut away any edge fabric that may be visible on the bottom. If the motifs are shaped, the end of the garment such as a wrap or hem will have a scalloped edge. Experiment by using feathers as a luxurious trimming (refer to Chiffon Wrap Edged with Throwster, page 91).

Consider using this technique around the hemline of an organza or chiffon dress or skirt.

Copacabana—fantasy headpiece made with bombyx silk, embellished with metallic threads, beads, sequins and feathers. The eyepiece has been machine embroidered and beaded.
55 cm (21½ in) wide inclusive of feathers

Using a satay stick

The technique of using a satay stick to change the direction of the fibres in your silk 'paper' can be worked using tussah, bombyx or throwster, or a combination. It can be done in straight rows, angled, vertical or in diagonally worked rows. Experiment using a circular motion.

Lay down a single layer of tops, alternating rows of tussah (or bombyx) with rows of throwster. The rows do not have to be of even width—some variation in the size will add interest to the design.

Continue laying down the fibres until the desired size is reached. This method lends itself well to hangings and edgings and wearables.

Opposite: Sample. Red/purple bombyx manipulated with a satay stick before wetting down. Slightly diluted Textile Medium gave a soft feel without losing any of the strength of the finished batt.

Left: Red/purple Throwster thinly laid, then manipulated with a satay stick before wetting down. The contrasting background emphasises the pattern of the manipulated silk fibres.

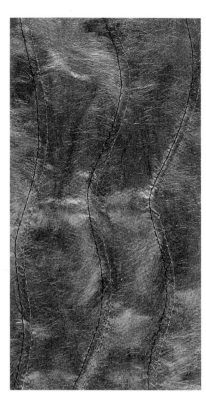

Above: Detail of yellow/gold bombyx bonded onto purple silk organza.

Above right: Sample. Brown throwster on a silk chiffon background. Free machine stitching and beading added when the silk was dry.

Wet the fibres with detergent and if you would like the project to be quite delicate and soft, slightly dilute the Textile Medium. Remember to apply detergent and medium to both sides.

Carefully remove the top layer of net. Using a satay stick or chopstick, move the wet fibres around, mixing the two silks together into waves and openwork. Once you have remodelled the fibres to your satisfaction, leave the silk on the bottom layer of net to dry on the frame.

Once you gain experience you can try manipulating the silk fibres before wetting down. This will result in a smooth surface but does take some time and patience. Once the silk has dried you can rewet and restyle it to add further texture. Experiment! Finally, add some beads or sequins as highlights on the dried piece.

Adding impact to a project

There are a myriad decorative elements available that can be used to add impact to a project and change the appearance of the silk 'paper' without detracting from its beauty.

Feathers It is not at all difficult to dye white or light-coloured feathers to tone or contrast with the silk 'paper'. Emu feathers are good if you can get hold of them, but failing that, craft shops are a good source of feathers suitable for dying.

Beading A popular method for adding light and emphasis to small areas of work. There are exciting sequins to be found, especially the exotic square ones now available. A delicate finish to a purse could be a purchased beaded fringe, or a purchased braid that can be embellished with beads to complement the colours of the work. There is a wide range of colourful beads available; you could also paint some small flat wooden beads with textile paints for added interest or make your own from 'paper' or rolled fabric. When stitching close to beads, use the machine zipper foot. This makes it easier to manoeuvre around them and will prevent needles being broken.

Fabrics Silk velvet, organza and chiffon, when used as appliqué, all blend well when combined with rich threads and woven cords.

Tassels of all descriptions can add the finishing touch to many pieces of work. These can be made by hand, or with the sewing machine. Use wools, DMC threads that come in varying thicknesses, rayon and silk, especially metallic threads to add that extra pizzazz. Think beyond threads, to torn strips of fabric to make tassels. Experiment by hanging buttons and beads from them. Purchase strands of beads and thin ribbons that can be turned into unusual tassels. I have a tassel made from leftover pieces of rayon cords, lengths of textured wools, and metallic rayons from which I have hung painted beads. All these were bits saved from my workroom 'savings box'.

Hand stitching Simple running stitch and thick silk threads add a soft and delicate texture to a surface. A toning colour will blend in with the background, a contrasting colour will help to emphasise a particular area of the design. See the hanging 'Reparation' opposite.

A selection of emu feathers hand-dyed by the author, has been used in these illustrations.

Opposite: Reparation
52 x 55 cm (20½ x 21½ in)
Hanging. Bombyx and throwster silk, appliqué, twin needle stitching, applied silk organza, hand stitching using silk threads.

Metallic threads A wide range of metallic threads is available, and they can be found in all thicknesses and weights, from fine machine embroidery threads in plain and variegated colours, to those that are too thick to pass through the machine needle but can be used on the bobbin. Many can be used in hand sewing with the use of a large-eyed needle. Metallics make a great addition to machine-made cords when used in straps for bags and purses. When sewing silk 'paper' it is advisable to sew with a slightly longer stitch than you would normally use with conventional fabric.

Braids Ready-made braids from home decor shops can be enriched with beads, bugle beads and sequins in matching or toning colours. If the braid is to be stitched to the opening of the purse, it is important that a strong thread is used when sewing on the beads. This will prevent them coming loose when the purse is handled. When stitching close to braids, use the machine zipper foot. This makes it easier to manoeuvre around the beads and will prevent needles being broken.

Space-dyed rayon ribbon is a very narrow rayon (sometimes silk) flat ribbon that has been dyed using two or more colours.

Materials and equipment for making up projects

- Sewing machine—serviced and cleaned regularly, extension lead, machine manual
- Accessory box, good lighting
- Open embroidery foot, darning foot and zipper foot
- Machine needles, sizes 10, 12, 14 (70, 80, 90)
- Twin needles, in selection of widths and weights
- Embroidery scissors with sharp points
- Scissors for cutting silk 'paper'
- Long sharp pins
- Tape measure
- Machine embroidery threads, plain and variegated and metallics
- Selection of beads and sequins
- Bead tray—an artist's palette is suitable for this purpose
- Beading thread, beading needles
- Hand sewing threads—-cotton, silk, rayon, in varying thicknesses and weights
- Containers for solutions—yoghurt pots or takeaway containers
- Rags, old towels, for cleaning work area
- Inexpensive bowls/containers in interesting shapes, plastic or glass (don't use your best ones for moulding the wet silk)
- Small metal measuring gauge
- Cutting board
- Sharp rotary cutter or craft knife
- Stiff cardboard for tassel making

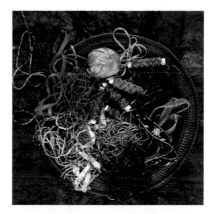

Opposite: Red/purple selection of beads, braids, sequins, threads, wools, cords and feathers for adding impact.

Top: Blue/emerald/lime selection of beads, braids, sequins, threads, wools, cords and feathers for adding impact.

Above: A selection of beads and sequins. An artist's palette of colours.

Above: Orange/red/gold selection of beads, braids, sequins, threads, wools, cords and feathers for adding impact.

Opposite: Some equipment I just can't do without! Measuring gauge, white pencil, twin needle, open embroidery foot, metallic pens, embroidery scissors with fine points.

- Selection of feathers—I have been using emu feathers which dye easily
- Dyes for feathers—feathers take most dyes easily, try dylon
- Satay sticks—they save the fingers when machine stitching and are useful for manipulating the surface
- Eye-dropper for measuring water when diluting medium
- Fine fuse wire
- Selection of silks, satins or other rich fabrics for lining bags and purses (look for remnants on sale tables)
- Cartridge paper for preparing patterns
- Vliesofix, a double-sided fusible web, ideal for all forms of appliqué, especially where small pieces are involved
- Velcro, a fastening with two components: a strip with tiny 'teeth ' that adheres to a fuzzy-backed strip and can be cut to size
- Selection of purchased braids and cords—a good selection can now be found at home decor stores
- Ribbons—rayon, silk, decorative wools, embroidery floss, metallic yarns
- Files/folders for retaining samples

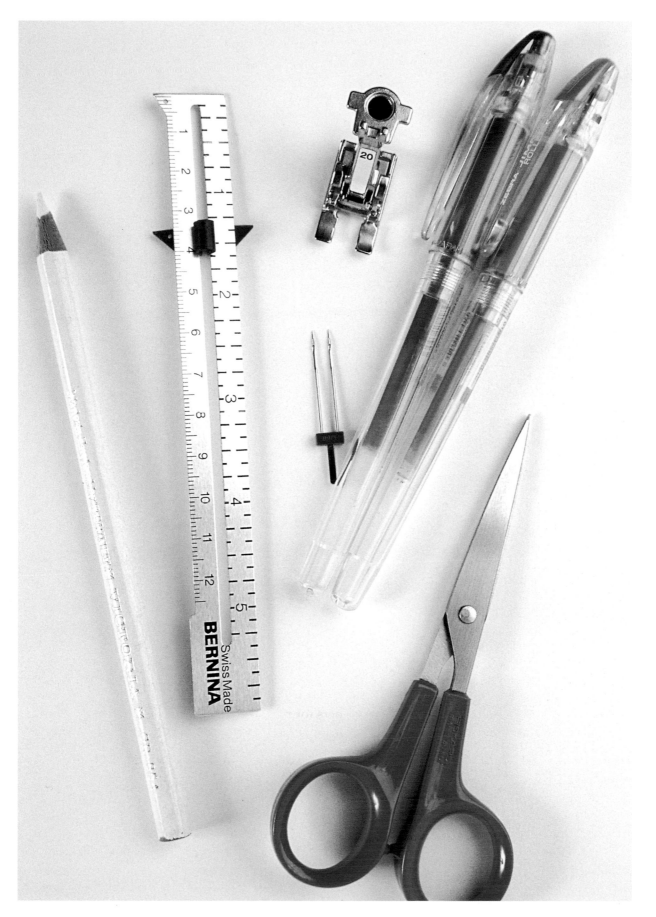

Things I just can't do without

- Sharp-pointed embroidery scissors
- Anti-static spray
- Vliesofix
- White marking pencil, metallic pens
- Notebook and pen beside my sewing machine and work table
- Machine manual
- Pins, wherever I happen to be working
- Magnetic bobbin holder and magnetic pin tray
- Needle threader
- Good lighting when sewing
- Metal measuring gauge

Useful tips

Have you got enough silk for your project?

To avoid the risk of running out of 'paper' when you come to cut out a pattern, try this idea when laying down the silk. Place the proposed pattern beneath the plastic sheet and the net to use as a guide to the finished size of the batt. Remove the pattern before wetting down the silk fibres. Remember to extend the silk fibres approximately 4–5 cm (2 in) beyond the outline of the pattern.

It can be useful to prepare enough 'paper' to make more than one item, so consider this when deciding how big to make the sheet of 'paper'.

Cutting and pinning

You cannot pin silk 'paper' to a pattern in the same way as conventional fabric. Place the 'paper' to be cut on a firm padded surface, such as an ironing board, and lay the pattern over it. Push the pins about halfway through the pattern and 'paper' into the padded surface, close to the edge of the pattern and angling the tips of the pins towards the centre. Angling the pins this way means you are less likely to catch them with the scissors. This method holds 'paper' and pattern together firmly enough to cut accurately.

Sewing a straight line—keeping your eye in

When sewing a straight line don't watch the needle, but direct your eyes ahead of it to the point where the line is going to finish. If you watch the needle and the foot, your eyes become distracted from guiding the needle in a straight line.

Sewing with machine needles

The surface of silk 'paper' is similar to paper in that a needle with a big eye will leave unsightly hole-marks in it. The most suitable needle sizes are 12 and 14 (80 and 90) which don't leave visible holes. You can always break the rules. If you need to make holes big enough to thread fine threads through, use a size 16 (100).

Threads

Machine embroidery threads are considerably thinner than general sewing threads and are more suitable for use on silk 'paper'. In working free machine embroidery it is easier to build up layers of threads for surface texture using finer threads.

Remember to slightly loosen the top tension to prevent the spool thread breaking. All thread tensions vary slightly, so you will need to experiment to find the tension which works best for your machine.

Making marks on the 'paper'

When marking pattern guidelines, use a sharpened white pencil or metallic pen. The colour of pen you choose will depend on the background colour of the 'paper'.

Producing smooth silk 'paper'

If your project requires a smooth sheet of 'paper', as for a book cover, purse, or a box, it is important that the plastic and net are absolutely smooth before you begin to lay down the silk fibres. After the wet silk and net have been placed on the drying frame, use your hands to carefully smooth out any ripples that may be visible. If there is still some surface unevenness after the silk has dried, press the 'paper' using a pressing cloth, brown paper or transparent baking paper placed between the iron and the 'paper'. Use a medium to hot iron. This should fix the problem.

Moulding and shaping

It can sometimes be difficult to hold a shape in place when drying the wet silk, especially when using the hairdryer. Clothes pegs are very useful for containing the shape in these cases.

Useful techniques

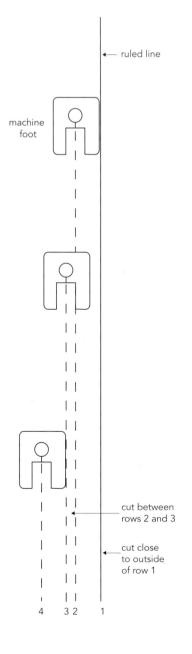

machine
foot

← ruled line

cut between
rows 2 and 3

← cut close
to outside
of row 1

4   3 2   1

Preparing strips for lattice work

You will need a three-layered sheet of 'paper'. The size of the 'paper' will depend on the project you have in mind.

Begin on the right-hand side of the sheet and, using a white pencil or metallic biro (depending on the colour of the 'paper'), rule a line the length of the 'paper'. The edge will not be very strong so you will need to come in approximately 3.5 cm (1⅜ in) to start.

Row 1 Using machine embroidery thread on the bobbin and spool, loosen the top tension to prevent the thread breaking, and lengthen the stitch. A slightly longer stitch than you would use in regular sewing is more suited for sewing silk 'paper'. Machines will vary for this adjustment, so you will have to experiment. Stitch down the ruled line. This will be the first guideline.

Row 2 Position the right-hand side of the machine foot (as it faces you) on the beginning of the stitched line. Using this line as a guide, stitch the second line.

Row 3 Position the inside of the right section of the machine foot on the beginning of the second line and stitch down the 'paper'. This makes a narrow channel to cut through.

Row 4 Position the outside of the foot on the beginning of the third row, stitch.

There will now be four rows of stitching.

Carefully cut between rows 2 and 3 as shown on the diagram—this will be your first strip. Cut away the excess 'paper' from the outer edge, close to the outside of the first row.

As you continue to stitch and cut, you will be working with only three rows of stitching, as the fourth row is only necessary on the first cut to remove the outer edge of the 'paper'. If you would like the strips to be narrower, place the right-hand side of the machine foot (as the foot faces you) on the outer cut edge instead of the stitched line.

Continue to stitch and cut until you have the required number of strips.

This method of stitching, using the machine foot as your guide, will enable you to stitch regular, straight lines that can be used for latticed or basket projects.

Determine the length of the strips according to the size of your motif, and, using an under and over technique, weave the strips together. Stitch around the outside edges. A few random stitches over the motif will be adequate to hold the strips in place.

The motif is now ready to be applied.

Vertical vessel. Woven strips of silk 'paper' made from bombyx silk.
40 cm high x 7 cm diameter (16 x 3 in)

Simple shoulder cords

A cut length of 110 cm (43 in) is adequate for most shoulder cords. It is a good idea to take a measurement over your shoulder before cutting the cord, remembering to include an allowance for the ends that will be stitched inside the purse. The length of the shoulder cord will depend on your height, and where you prefer the bag to sit. You might like to test with a piece of string to establish the most suitable length.

There is a good selection of unusual ready-made textured cords and interesting wools available from home decorating stores and shops supplying knitting wools.

If you wish to make your own shoulder cord, there are lots of possibilities:

1   Take two lengths of braid, approximately 2.5 cm (1 in) wide, wrong sides facing, and stitch down both long sides with matching thread. This cord can be used as is, or wool can be threaded through the tube to make it thicker. Use a safety pin to run the wool through the tube.

2   Sew a thin tube of silk or some other rich fabric, turn, and using thick wool and a large-eyed needle with a blunt point, thread some thick wool through the tube. This method makes a soft, light cord.

3   A machine-stitched cord can be made quite easily by laying three, four or five lengths of fine cords, ribbons or textured wools together. The number of lengths required will depend on

the thickness of the yarns used. Tie a knot at one end of the threads/wools/ribbons and use the machine running stitch—this is similar to the satin stitch but rounded. Lengthen the stitch to ensure that the stitches do not flatten or cover the strands of the cord. Begin stitching along the cords/ribbons, holding the short end with the left hand and twisting the long ends of the cords with the right hand as you sew. If the materials you are using are on a ball or cone, do not cut off the lengths until you have sewn the required size.

4   Using a very close satin stitch (zig-zag), an open embroidery or cording foot and machine embroidery threads, you can sew over thin wool and make several fine cords that can be twisted together. Metallic machine threads will add richness.

5   For a twisted cord made by hand you can use almost any type of yarn such as silk, wool, fine ribbons, metal threads, thin strips of leather, even narrow torn strips of fabric. Select the yarns and group them together. Each length of yarn should be three times the required length of the finished cord.

6   Knot a loop at each end and slip one end over a hook or door handle. Slip a pencil through the other tied end. Standing away from the door or hook, ensure that the yarns are taut and begin to twist the pencil round and round. When the yarns are tight enough they will begin to twist and curl. Establish the centre and place a weight, such as the hook of a coathanger, over the twisting yarns. Remember to keep the threads very taut before they begin to twist or they will wind unevenly. Now, let the yarns double over themselves, starting from the centre where the weight is. Knot the twisted ends—the knots can be undone prior to fixing the cord to the project.

Projects

Notecard sachet

WITH LATTICE MOTIF

Materials

- Sheet of 3-layered silk 'paper', approximately 40 x 50 cm (15½ x 19½ in), made with tussah or bombyx and Textile Medium (press the 'paper' before cutting out the pattern)
- Sewing machine, presser foot, open embroidery foot
- Machine needles, size 12 (80)
- Machine embroidery threads to match or tone with your chosen silk
- Heavy 'paper' or light vilene for the pattern
- Embroidery scissors with sharp points, long sharp pins
- Sharp scissors to cut silk 'paper'
- 1 m (1 yd) narrow ribbon for tie
- Matching or toning notecards and envelopes

Method

1   Cut a pattern using heavy 'paper' or vilene. Mark in stitching and pressing lines. The pattern will have to be enlarged by 163%. For your reference, the pressing lines have been indicated by stitching in the diagram on page 76.

2   Select the preferred sides of the 'paper' for front and back and pin the pattern to the 'paper'. The silk 'paper' may be too thick to push the pins through in the conventional way. Push the pin at least halfway through the 'paper' and pattern towards the centre of the work. This prevents contact with the scissors when cutting out, but is enough to hold the work together for cutting (see Cutting and pinning, page 65).

3   Cut out the pattern.

Opposite: Notecard sachet, with motif and ribbon tie.

Previous pages: Sea urchins made in bombyx silk with Acrylic Gloss medium. Each urchin was constructed from a square of 'paper'. The four points of the square were gathered to form a central point, which was then secured with a strong thread. The form was then shaped before beading.

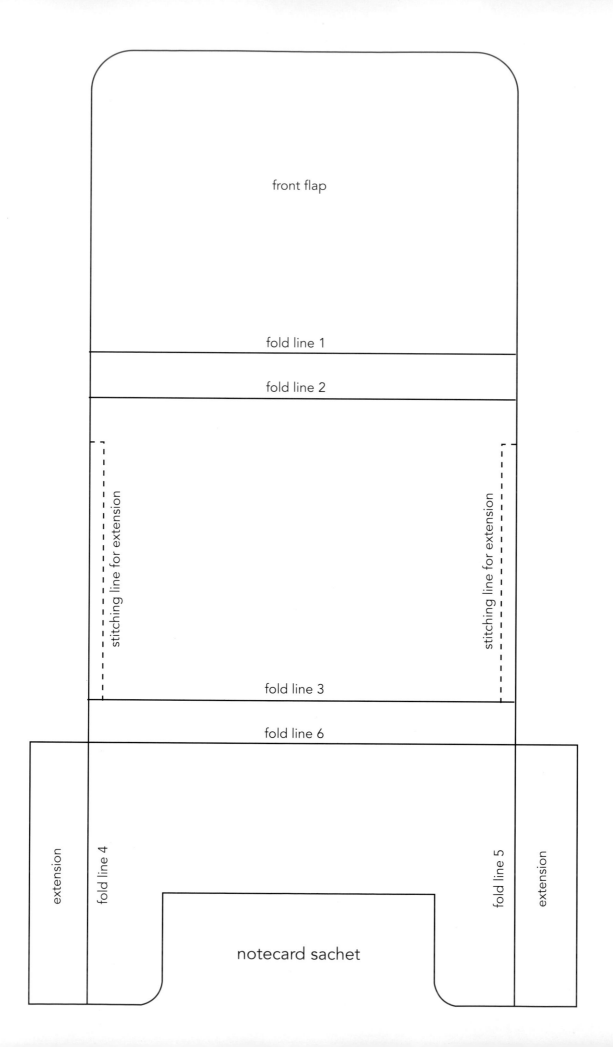

4   Ensure that the machine is clean and insert a new needle. Select the machine embroidery thread which can be either a toning or a contrasting colour, thread the spool and insert the bobbin. Reduce the top tension and lengthen the stitch.

5   Stitch twice around the outside edge of the sachet. Mark the fold lines (pressing lines) from the pattern. You can do this by pushing pins through the pattern. Press the seams on the outside of the sachet. If you would like to define the fold lines, stitch along each one after pressing.

6   Should you wish to add a label, stitch it to the front of the front flap or on the inside of the front flap. Do this before attaching the motif.

Prepare the lattice motif

Following the procedure described on page 68, first cut a square of 'paper' approximately 15 cm (6 in) square from which to cut the strips to make the motif.

The size and shape of the motif will your choice. The motif in the photo is only a guide. Once the strips have been cut, work them into a lattice pattern and stitch around the outer edge to contain the pieces.

7   Position the motif on the outside of the front flap. Attach to the sachet by a single row of stitches just inside the edge of the motif.

Assembling the sachet

1   With right side of the work facing you, turn in flap on fold
    lines 4 and 5. Fold the extensions of fold lines 4 and 5 back
    to meet fold line 3.

2   Stitch the extensions of fold lines 4 and 5 to sides of sachet
    between fold lines 3 and 2.

3   Insert matching or toning notecards and envelopes and tie
    the ribbon around the sachet.

NB This pattern can be enlarged to make a clutch bag.

Opposite: Notecard sachet in progress.
Shows shape cut ready to be sewn and
strips of silk 'paper' being assembled
for the lattice motif.

Drawstring receptacle
THROWSTER ON SILK ORGANZA

Materials

- Small quantity of throwster fibres (about a fistful)
- ½ m (½ yd) silk, rayon or metallic organza for receptacle
- ½ m (½ yd) silk, rayon or metallic organza for lining
- Sewing machine, presser foot, zipper foot, darning foot
- Machine needles, size 10 or 12 (70 or 80)
- Machine embroidery threads in plains and metallics
- Sharp scissors to cut the silk 'paper'
- Embroidery scissors
- Long sharp pins
- Heavy paper or thin vilene for pattern
- 15 cm (6 inches) beaded trim
- Beads, sequins
- 1 m (1 yd) narrow ribbon, plain or space-dyed

The finished size of the receptacle is 23 x 14.5 cm (9 x 5½ in) inclusive of the 'frilly' top edge and beaded trim. A seam allowance of approximately 5 mm (¼ in) is included on the pattern. Remember, press 'paper' made using Textile Medium before commencing to sew.

Opposite: Drawstring receptacle made from throwster bonded onto silk organza using textile medium.
14 x 20 cm (5½ x 8 in)

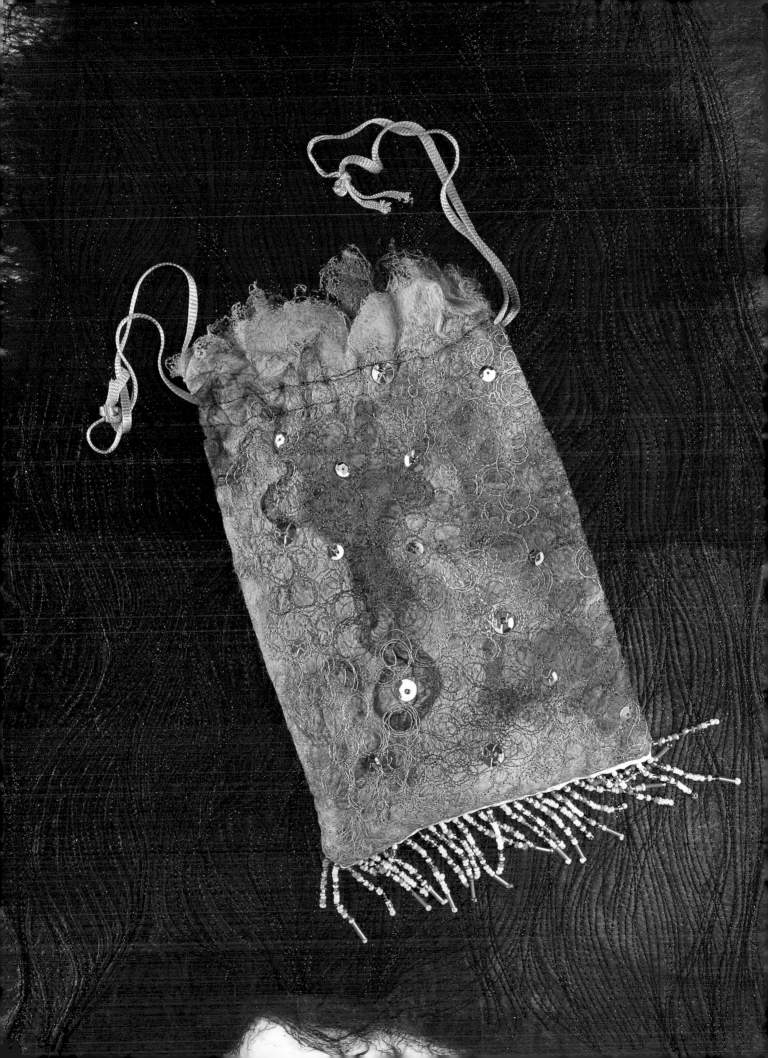

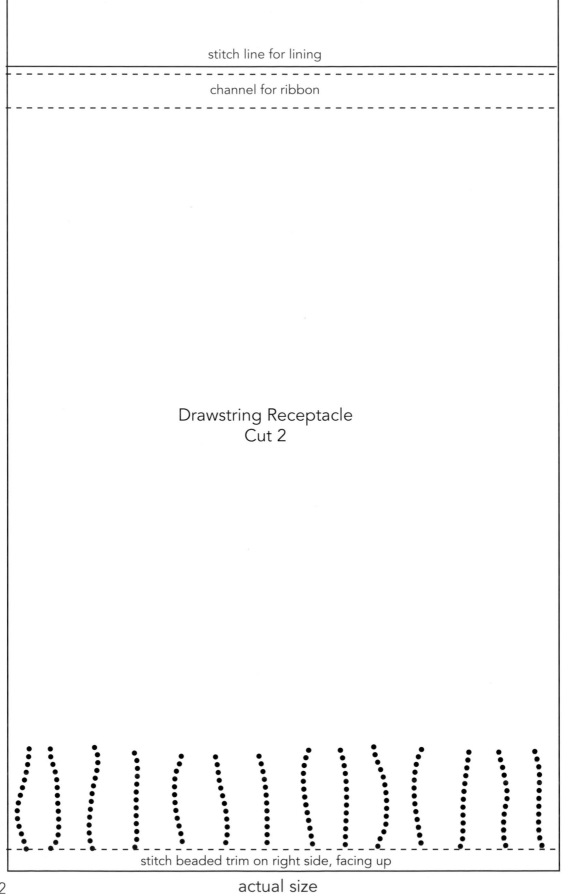

throwster border extends beyond lining

stitch line for lining

channel for ribbon

Drawstring Receptacle
Cut 2

stitch beaded trim on right side, facing up

actual size

Method

Lay down the plastic, net and organza backing, approximately 25 cm (10 in) square.

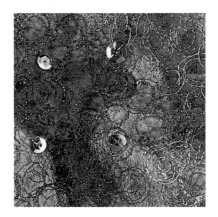

Pull apart the throwster until it resembles fine lace-like threads. Cover the organza fabric background with the fibres. Some of the background can show through if you wish.

I extended the edge fibres approximately 4 cm (1½ in) beyond the fabric on one long side. This is how the soft top edge was obtained. As you are using only a single layer of fibres, once you are happy with the arrangement, place a layer of net over the top and wet down with detergent and water, then some lightly diluted Textile Medium. Remember to wet down both sides of the work, including the organza.

Leave the fibres and organza to dry on a frame. Because the fibres are laid down thinly, the work will dry quickly.

When dry, remove the net from both sides but retain the organza. If you are using silk organza, the throwster fibres will adhere well. It does not adhere to rayon quite as readily, but any loose fibres can be contained by stitching.

Because a background fabric has been used, it is possible to work free machine embroidery without using a frame. Using the darning foot, and machine embroidery thread in the bobbin and on the spool, slightly loosen the top tension and work free machine embroidery in a circular motion over the piece.
A combination of plain and metallic threads will add light and dark areas to the surface.

Use the pattern to cut the front and back pieces; the top edges will have the extended edge without the fabric.

Select beads or sequins and attach them randomly to add emphasis to the circular stitching.

Adding the beaded fringe

Pin the ribbon of the beaded trim to the outside (the throwster side) bottom edge of one piece, with the beaded fringe facing towards the top of the receptacle. This will be easier if you first tack the beaded trim to the background.

Using the zipper foot, stitch approximately 5 mm (¼ in) from the beads, or as close as you can manage.

Stitching sides and base together

With right sides together and the beaded fringe inside towards the centre, pin the sides and base together. It will be easier if you tack the pieces before stitching. Using the presser foot, stitch down the sides, then change to the zipper foot and carefully stitch across the bottom edge. Using the zipper foot will enable you to stitch close to the beads.

Opposite: Sample. Thinly laid turquoise bombyx silk with free machine stitching using plain and metallic threads. Even although the silk has been thinly laid it is possible, with care, to work free machine stitching without using a frame.

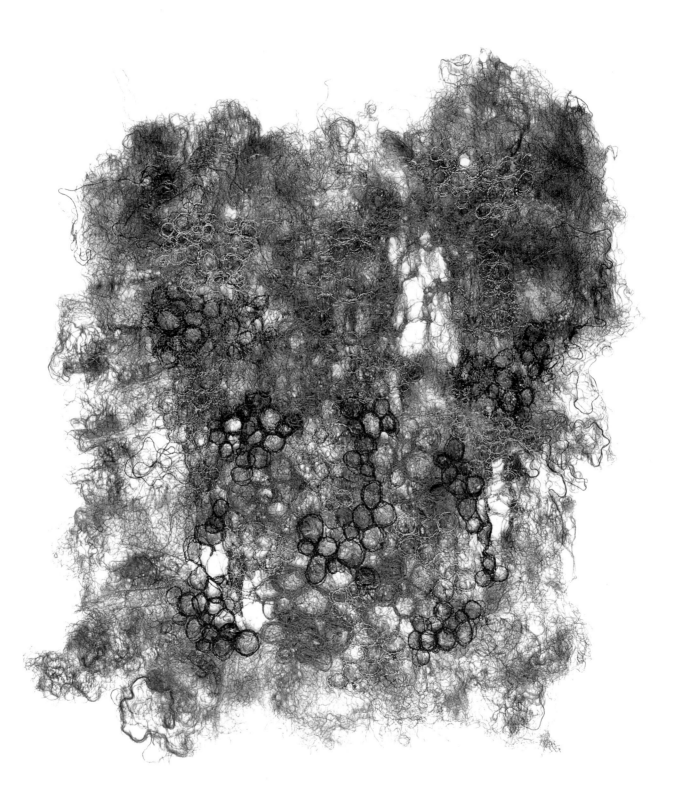

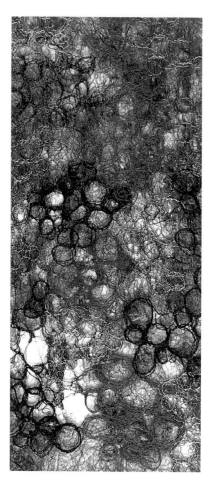

Turn the work. You will have the seams inside and the beaded trim will be hanging from the base of the receptacle.

Lining and finishing

Cut two lining pieces 15 x 22 cm (6 x 8½ in) and stitch sides and bottom, with a 1 cm (⅜ in) seam.

Turn down a 1 cm (⅜ in) hem on the top of the lining, stitch.

Position the lining inside the receptacle, the seams of the lining facing the seams of the receptacle.

Place the bag and lining through the free arm of the machine. Using the presser foot, sew a channel approximately 1 cm (⅜ in) wide around the top of the lining and bag. Carefully make a small opening on either side of the bag on the outside and thread the ribbon through the channel using a small safety pin. Knot the ends of the ribbon.

Bougainvillea basket

Working with a three-layered sheet of 'paper' made from bombyx silk tops in vibrant bougainvillea colours, 55 cm (21½ in) square, and using Acrylic Gloss medium, 64 strips of 'paper' approximately 8 mm (⁵⁄₁₆ in) wide were cut using the method discussed on page 75.

Bougainvillea basket.
27 cm square x 14 cm deep
(10½ x 5 inches)

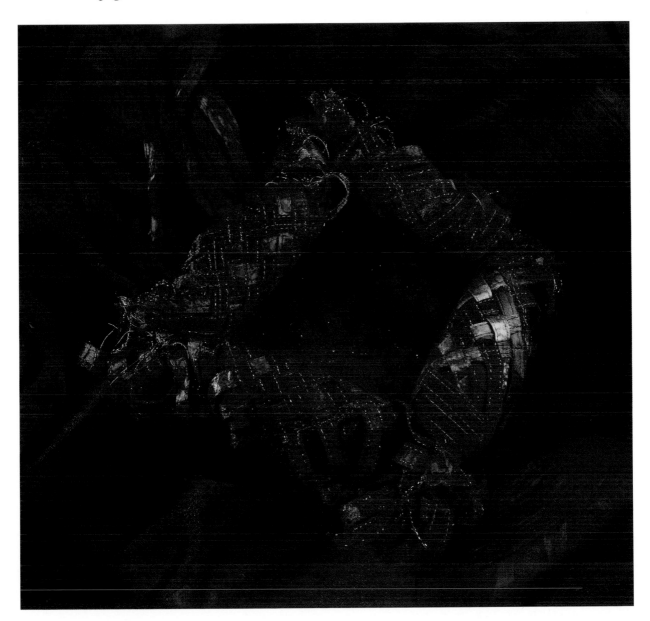

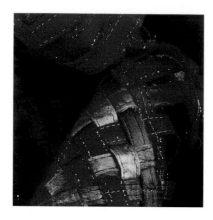

The strips were divided into two lots for verticals and horizontals, and woven into a square lattice.

After weaving the basket shape (the sides were rolled as the base was drying), it was obvious it was not yet stiff enough to be free standing and that more Acrylic Gloss needed to be added to the dry silk 'paper' lattice-work. When drying the basket lay a pad of newspapers on the work table to soak up any excess liquid.

The basket was lightly wetted down using a brush and water, then extra medium was applied both inside and out.

Drape the wet silk on the outside of a square ice-cream container. Place a jar or jug on the table (on the newspaper) and stand the upturned container and wet silk on top of the jar. This acts as a trivet to lift the container and wet silk above the table and makes the drying process much easier. The basket can be dried to stiffness using a hairdryer set at medium/high. Clothes pegs helped to keep ends and edges in position during drying.

Lastly, the free ends of the strips were painted with more Acrylic Gloss, then dried while curled around my fingers to roll up the four sides.

It took four hours to stitch and cut the strips, and three and a half hours to weave them together—not a quick project, but rewarding when finished!

Silk chiffon wrap
WITH THROWSTER MOTIFS AND BEADS

Materials

- 2 m (2 yd) silk chiffon in your choice of colour (silk chiffon is very easy to dye, so if you are unable to find the colour you like, do not despair, just dye some in your favourite colour, or ask a friend to dye it for you in exchange for some lustrous silk 'paper'!)
- Small quantity of throwster
- Detergent, water, eye-dropper
- Containers for detergent and medium
- Textile medium
- Plastic sheet, net, brushes
- Bonding powder, plastic spoon for applying the powder
- Iron, press cloth or clear baking paper
- Sewing machine, darning foot, presser foot
- Machine embroidery threads
- Beads
- Scissors, long sharp pins
- Beading needle, beading thread

Top: Working sample for lilac chiffon wrap, with motifs being applied to the edge.

Above: Lilac chiffon wrap, with embroidered and beaded motifs applied to both sides of the ends and to the centre of the back on both sides. 2 m x 1 m (2 yd x 1 yd)

Method

1   Prepare the throwster motifs as described on page 50. They can be in colourways from light to dark of the one colour, or a variety of colours that tone with the chiffon.

2   The motifs are applied to both ends and both sides of the wrap. You can also include a smattering of them scattered randomly over the centre back. For the wrap in these pictures, approximately 24 were used at each end, on both sides, a total of 96 (48 for each end), plus another ten or so which I placed in the centre back on both sides. The final number will be a personal choice.

3   Lay one end of the chiffon on a flat surface and arrange 24 of the motifs to your liking, remembering to overlap some slightly at the raw edge of the chiffon at the cut end. To prevent the chiffon moving while you are placing the motifs, lay it on a cloth or ironing board. Remember to test the background fabric for heat suitability before ironing.

4   Once you have decided on the pattern, carefully pin the motifs to the chiffon, using a single pin positioned vertically. Working with one motif at a time, lift the first one and, placing a small quantity of bonding powder in a spoon, gently tap a sprinkling of powder onto the fabric. Position the motif over the bonding powder and carefully remove the pin. Using a medium to hot iron and a press cloth or transparent baking paper (which enables you to see exactly where the motif is), bond the motif to the chiffon. Repeat this procedure until all the motifs have been applied to this side of the end of the wrap.

Lilac wrap with embroidered and
beaded throwster motifs.
2 m x 1 m (2 yd x 1 yd)

5   Turn the chiffon over and repeat the process. It is not necessary to match the motifs front to back. They will overlap in places, and in others there will be spaces leaving a shadow effect showing through the chiffon. This adds to the interest of the design.

6   Repeat the process on the other end of the wrap, bonding motifs to both sides, then, if you wish, a few motifs to the centre of the wrap, again on front and back.

7   Using the darning foot, with machine embroidery thread in the bobbin and on the spool, work random circles of stitching through all the motifs. With careful handling, it should not be necessary to frame the work. If you wish, connect some of the motifs with random stitching; this adds to the overall effect of the embellishment. The thread I used was varied, pale pink on one side and pale lilac on the other.

8   Finally, using very sharp-pointed embroidery scissors, carefully trim away any raw edges of chiffon showing between the overlapped motifs at the ends of the wrap, which will take on a scalloped effect.

9   Using a selection of small beads in toning or contrasting colours, add highlights to both sides of selected motifs. It is not necessary to add beads to all the motifs—only a small number of beads are required. Don't forget to include some on the centre back motifs.

Theatre purse

WITH TWIN NEEDLE STITCHING, FEATHERS, BEADED BRAID TRIM

Materials

- A three-layered sheet of silk 'paper' approximately 40 x 50 cm (15½ x 19½ inches) made using Textile Medium
- Approximately 0.5 m (½ yd) lining fabric (I used a silk remnant)
- Thick paper or light vilene for pattern, pen for drawing up patterns
- Sewing machine, presser foot, open embroidery foot, zipper foot
- Machine needles, 10, 12 (70, 80)
- Twin needle, 90 x 4.0 mm is a suitable size
- Machine embroidery threads, plain and metallics
- Scissors, pins, tape measure, white pencil for marking pattern lines
- 0.5 m (½ yd) purchased narrow braid
- 1 m (1 yd) either ready-made cord or textured wools, narrow ribbon or glitzy threads to make a shoulder cord (remember to check length of cord)
- Feathers, beads
- PVA glue
- Cotton buds for applying glue

Remember to press any 'paper' made using Textile Medium before beginning to stitch.

Method

1   Use the thick paper or vilene to draw up the pattern for the purse and inside pocket, marking in the details shown on the pattern. The pattern will be enlarged to 140%.

2   With sharp scissors, cut one front and one back from the silk 'paper'.

3   Using a single needle, the presser foot or open embroidery foot, and machine embroidery thread on the spool and in the bobbin, slightly loosen the top tension and with a lengthened stitch sew right around the outside of both purse pieces, close to the edge. Work two rows of stitching around both front and back.

4   Change to twin needles and thread up the machine as under Twin needles in the Glossary. Plain thread and a metallic could be used, or variegated and plain, or two plains—the choice is yours. When choosing thread colours, consider the colour of the braid and feathers you will be using to trim the purse and, of course, the colour of the purse itself.

5   Follow the outline of the purse to contour the lines of twin needle stitching, using the needles as a gauge for the space between the rows.

Beaded and feathered theatre purse.
22 x 19 cm (8½ x 7½ in)

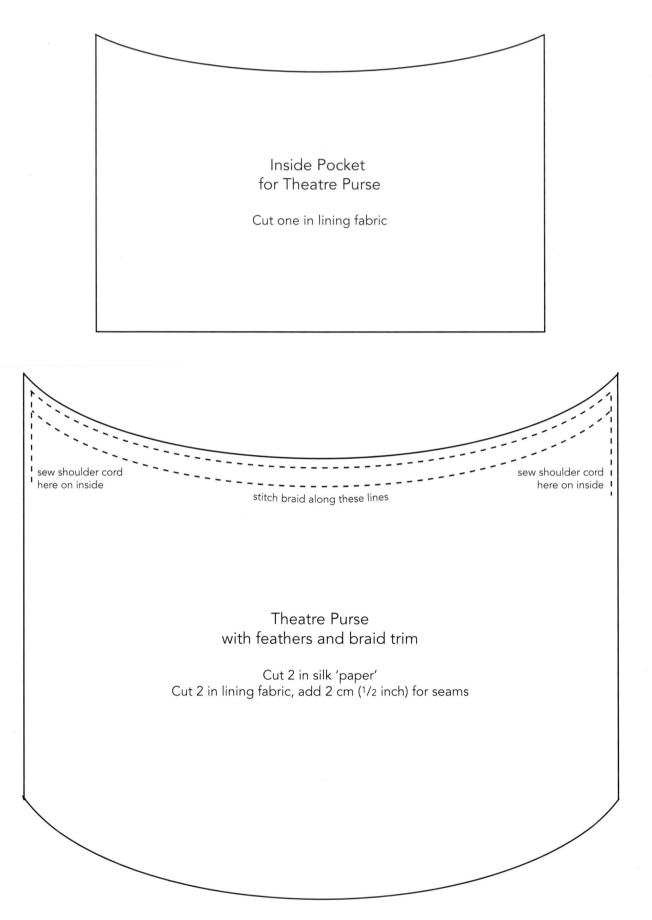

Inside Pocket
for Theatre Purse

Cut one in lining fabric

sew shoulder cord
here on inside

sew shoulder cord
here on inside

stitch braid along these lines

Theatre Purse
with feathers and braid trim

Cut 2 in silk 'paper'
Cut 2 in lining fabric, add 2 cm (1/2 inch) for seams

Inserting the shoulder cord

1 Change back to the single needle. Whether you are using a ready-made cord, making your own following the instructions on page 70, stitch this in now.

2 Determine the length that suits you—usually 110 cm (approx. 43 in) is sufficient. Stitch the cord approximately 2.5 cm (1 in) down the inside of one side of the purse. Sew up and down 3 or 4 times, stitching as close to the edge as possible. Use a straight stitch. Make sure that the cord does not protrude from the side of the purse. Repeat on the other side. Any excess cord inside can be trimmed away when the stitching has been completed.

Lining

1 Cut one front, one back and one inner pocket from lining fabric. Add 1.5 cm (½ in) to the pattern for seams.

2 Turn the top edge of the inner pocket over approximately 1 cm (⅜ inch) and press the turned edges checking the fabric for heat compatibility first. Snip the inside curve very slightly, taking care not to cut too far into the pressed turning, to allow the edge to sit neatly. Machine around all sides using a matching thread.

3 Fold one of the purse lining pieces in half to establish the midline. Using a pin, mark 4 cm (1½ in) down from the top edge and pin the inner pocket to the right side of the lining.

4 Stitch around two sides and bottom of inner pocket. Take the stitching 3 or 4 stitches across the opening to reinforce the corners.

Feathered theatre purse in preparation.

5   If you use a name label, stitch this above the inner pocket on the lining.

6   With right sides together and inner pocket on the inside, stitch along the two sides and bottom edge of the lining. Press the top edge over twice, approximately 1.5 cm (½ in) in all, ready to be hand stitched into the purse.

Attaching the feathers

My early attempts at attaching feathers were not very successful. Eventually I discovered that to prevent them coming away from the stitching I had to glue them to the 'paper' before stitching.

Arrange the feathers on the bag front with the shafts of the feathers to the top edge. Use a strong glue such as PVA to carefully attach the feathers to the 'paper'. Using a cotton bud to apply the glue will help prevent any excess glue staining the purse. Press the shafts to the purse with your fingers, and keep pressure on for a minute or two. The feathers will adhere quickly. Do this on both pieces of the purse.

Once the glue has dried, trim away any shafts extending above the top edge of the pieces.

Stitch 2 or 3 times along the top of the feathers by machine. Machine embroidery thread is suitable for this.

Trimming—braid and beads

1   Add beads and/or sequins to the braid in colours to complement both it and the purse, in either contrasting or toning shades.

2   Pin the braid along the top edge of the purse front, covering the shafts of the feathers.

3   Take the cut ends of the braid over the sides of the purse and tuck inside about 1.5 cm (½ in). The excess can be cut away from the inside when you have stitched the braid to the purse. This is made easier if you first tack the braid to the purse.

4   Using the zipper foot, stitch along the top edge, down the sides, and along the bottom of the applied braid. The zipper foot affords a better view of the braid and beads and avoids the foot becoming in contact with the beads.

5   Repeat the procedure on the back of the purse.

Front to back

1   Pin front and back of the purse together. It will not be possible to get the pins through in the normal manner, but by pushing them in as far as they will go, the two sides will be held together sufficiently to begin stitching.

2   Begin machine stitching along the top opening, working 4 or 5 stitches to the outer edge. This extra stitching reinforces the corners. Continue stitching down the side of the purse, along the bottom edge, and along the second side. Finish with 4 or 5 stitches on the opposite side to reinforce the corners. Repeat this stitching process once more.

3   Trim away any excess braid from the inside of the purse.

Inserting the lining

Pin the lining to the inside of the purse. Hand stitch close to the top edge using small stitches.

Contributing artists

Nancy Ballesteros

'Sample'

33 x 41 cm (13 x 16 in)

This sample was felted by hand using fine merino wool tops and silk 'paper'.

The shapes were cut from silk 'paper' which was made using methylcellulose. This thick paste temporarily binds the silk together until it washes away during the felting process, wherein the wool fibres work through the silk just enough to bind it together.

Nancy has been working with felt making over the past ten years. She enjoys experimenting with new techniques and new fibre combinations. However, she mainly runs Treetops Colour Harmonies where she specialises in hand-dyeing mixed colourways on various silk fibres and fine merino wool.

Previous page: Tulip bowl. The outer edges are bound with torn strips of metallic fabric.
24 cm diameter x 18 cm deep
(9½ x 7 in)

Alvena Hall

'L'ill Wave' and 'Beach'

Top section 30 x 25 cm (11½ x 9½ in);
lower section 60 x 50 cm (23½ x 19½ in)

The construction of 'L'ill Wave' includes the use of water-soluble 'fabric' on the outer edges, machine-made embroidered lace and free hand stitching. Surface texture has been added with the appliqué of tiny fish and hand beading using shells and glass beads.

'Beach' has been embroidered with couched, hand-dyed rayon ribbons and hand and free machine embroidery, with the addition of shells and beads.

Alvena has not previously worked with silk 'paper' and she found it a very challenging and satisfying medium to extend her expertise in creating lace-like surfaces on textiles.

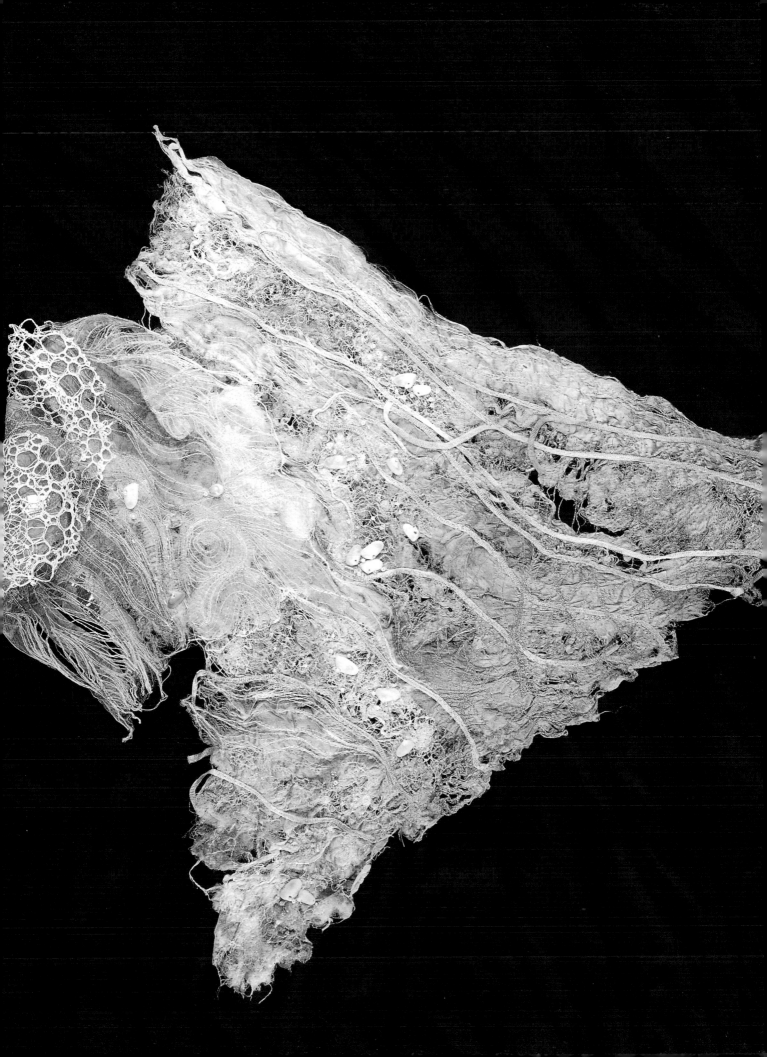

Lois Ives

'Old Gold' and 'Cyclamen'

Potpourri sachets, both 21 x 15 cm (8 x 6 in)

The silk 'paper' sachets are decorated with flowers made from silk throwster waste, Japanese braid and beads.

Lois makes accessories from silk 'paper' and silk felt, working with many kinds of threads that include silk. Needlelace, beads, hand-made braid, hand and machine embroidery are her favourite ways of decorating these accessories. Currently, Lois is working with braid and bead jewellery.

Sue Seaman

'Cloud Drift'

Silk chiffon stole with wool and silk tops and silk throwster waste felted into the chiffon

1080 x 90 cm (68 x 35 in)

Having spent over thirty years working with wool, both as a producer and a craftsperson, Sue's knowledge of the fibre is extensive. She has taught spinning, weaving, knitting and dyeing workshops over the years and was one of the first people to make felt in Australia. As a self-taught felter she had to experiment with ways to produce fine soft felt, and she has taught these techniques throughout Western Australia.

She now concentrates on felt-making. Sue produces a wide variety of articles, from sculptural pieces and wearable art, to soft, flowing evening wear. The excitement of dyeing her own fibres adds to her pleasure in marrying silk and wool to create her own individual style.

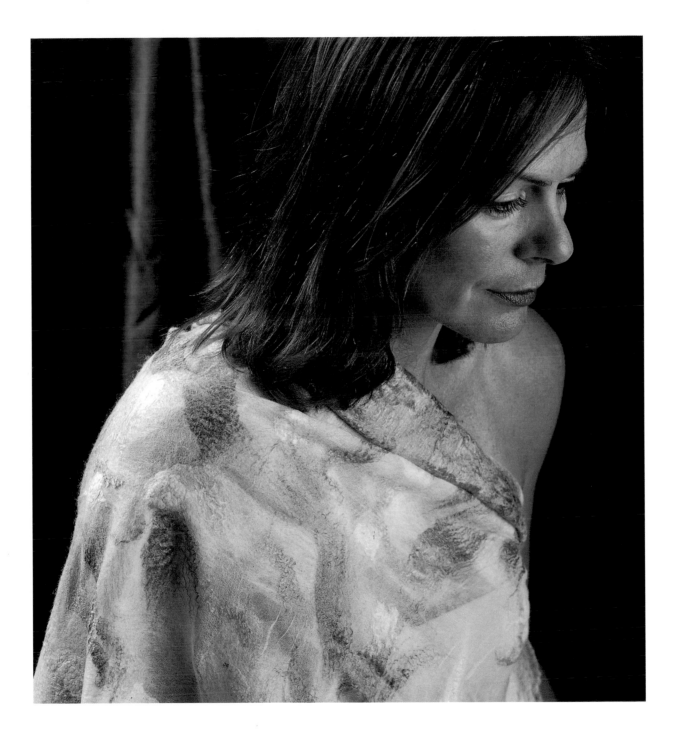

Glossary

Anti-static spray

Used to lightly spray silk tops and throwster to reduce static electricity and render the fibres more manageable. It is not necessary to totally wet the fibres, just spray lightly. Wait 6–7 minutes for the silk to dry. When dry, continue laying down the fibres.

Batt (or layer)

The silk tops that have been laid down to make a sheet of silk 'paper'. The 'paper' can consist of one, two or three layers or batts.

Bombyx mori

The domesticated silkworm, which produces white fibres of excellent quality. This silk is considered to be the finest silk available. Being white, bombyx silk is excellent for dyeing, and the colours produced are extremely pure and rich. The tops are thinner than tussah and therefore a little more difficult to use.

Laying down

The process used to prepare a sheet of silk 'paper' (refer to How to make silk 'paper').

'Paper'

Name given to the formed fibres when dry.

Raw silk

Silk that contains all its natural gum or sericin.

Snapping

Technique used with bombyx silk to open up and straighten the strands, smooth down any loose fibres and make the fibres more pliable. Hold the length of silk fibres with both hands as if preparing to pull out the fibres. Use both hands, carefully pulling the fibres to left and right at the same time.

Substrate

Base, underlayer or foundation on which to work.

Throwster silk

(or throwster waste)

The clean thread waste formed during the cleaning of the bombyx silk fibres. This waste is quite different in appearance to either tussah or bombyx silk. The fibres are very strong and bear a resemblance to merino fibres in parts. A different approach is required when laying down throwster, and owing to the strength of the threads it can be a much slower process than using tussah or bombyx silk. Throwster is particularly prone to developing static electricity and you will find that spraying with an anti-static solution enables the fibres to be controlled more easily.

Twin needles

Best described as one shank with two needles that use two reels of thread. The bobbin does not change. The needle fits into the machine like a single needle, and can be used on all machines. These needles are available in various widths, that is, the space between the two needles. The eye of the needle comes in sizes relating to conventional machine needles. I usually use a size 12 or 14 (80–90). A suitable width for sewing silk 'paper' is 4.0 mm. A 2.0 mm needle width gives a narrower channel between the two threads.

When threading the needles, take one thread through the left of the tension disc, then through to the needle on the left. The second thread goes to the right side of the tension disc and is threaded through the eye of the right needle. This prevents the two threads tangling during sewing.

Should you need to change direction when stitching with twin needles, never leave the needles in the work as is usual when using a single needle. Twin needles will break if you turn them in the fabric.

Ensure that the foot being used is wide enough to accommodate the width of the twin needles. Always centre the needles over the foot, otherwise they can hit the foot and break. Silk 'paper' lends itself very well to stitching with twin needles.

Tussah silk
Wild silk, which is coarser than cultivated silk. It is pale cream in colour and when dyed, the colours are not as intense as the bombyx silk. The texture is such that it is easy to pull out when preparing a batt.

Suppliers

Tussah, bombyx and throwster silk may be sourced from these suppliers.

AUSTRALIA

Treetops Colour Harmonies

www.treetopscolours.com.au

info@treetopscolours.com.au

6 Benwee Road

Floreat

WA 6014

tel + 61 8 9387 3007

fax + 61 8 9387 1747

also suppliers of medium

The Thread Studio

6 Smith Street

Perth

WA 6000

tel + 61 8 9227 1561

fax + 61 8 9227 0254

email:

mail@thethreadstudio.com

www.thethreadstudio.com

NORTH AMERICA

Treenway Silks

www.treenwaysilks.com

501 Musgrave Road

Salt Spring Island

BC

Canada V8K 1V5

toll free 1 888 383 7455

fax 250 653 2347

GREAT BRITAIN

The Handweavers Studio

www.handweaversstudio.co.uk

29 Haroldstone Road

London

UK E17 7AN

tel 020 8251 2281

NEW ZEALAND

Honora Undrill

email:

undrill@mlb.planet.gen.nz

Whareaton Farm

Howard Valley RDZ

Nelson

New Zealand

tel 0 64 3 521 1135

fax 64 3 521 1136